WELCOME TO THE WORLD OF

Snakes

Diane Swanson

Whitecap Books
Vancouver / Toronto

Edited by Elizabeth McLean
Cover design by Steve Penner
Interior design by Margaret Ng
Typeset by Maxine Lea
Cover photograph by Kitchin & Hurst/First Light
Photo credits: Wayne Lynch iv, 12, 14, 22, 26; Nate Kley 2; Mark Snyder, Natural Selections/First Light 4; B. Milne/First Light 6; A.B. Sheldon/Dembinsky Photo Assoc 8; Kenneth Krysko 10; Medford Taylor/First Light 16; Tim Christie/TimChristie.com 18; Joel Sartore/First Light 20; Natural Selections/First Light 24

Printed and bound in Canada

Canadian Cataloguing in Publication Data

Swanson, Diane, 1944–
    Welcome to the world of snakes

    Includes index.
    ISBN 1-55285-171-0

    1. Snakes—North America—Juvenile literature. I. Title.
QL666.O6592 2001   j597.96'097   C2001-910175-9

For more information on
this series and other
Whitecap Books titles,
visit our web site at
www.whitecap.ca

The publisher acknowledges the support of the Canada Council for the Arts and the Cultural Services Branch of the Government of British Columbia for our publishing program. We acknowledge the financial support of the Government of Canada through the Book Industry Development Program for our publishing activities.

Contents

World of Difference

S-S-SNAKES S-S-SIMPLY S-S-SLITHER. Having no legs, they get around just fine on their bellies. Their covering of scaly skin protects them from sharp rocks and rough sand. It keeps them from drying out, too. But a snake's skin is never slimy, as people often think.

Compared to most other animals, snakes have long, slender bodies. Some kinds also have special features. A horned rattlesnake has "horns" that prevent its eyes from getting covered when it buries itself in sand. A hognose snake has a turned-up nose that's useful in burrowing for food.

Like other snakes, this big boa constrictor is covered with tough scales.

1

No, it's not a worm—but a tiny thread snake, which burrows underground.

Of the 2500 to 3000 different kinds of snakes on Earth, about 500 live in North America. Some of the shortest are the skinny thread snakes—only 11 to 15 centimetres (4½ to 6 inches) in length. One of the longest snakes in North America—found in southern Mexico—is the boa constrictor. Although it often grows about 2 metres (6 feet) long, it can reach 5 metres (16½ feet)!

Many snakes are dull colors—brown, gray, and black. Blending in with rocks, sand, and branches, they're less likely to be noticed by their enemies, such as eagles and hawks. And the snakes can sneak up on animals they want to eat. The skin of the boa constrictor, for instance, is a mix of light and dark shades, which helps the snake hide in the flickering sunlight and shadows of the forest.

LEGGY SNAKE

In 2000, an international science team reported rediscovering the remains of a snake in a museum drawer in Jerusalem. About 95 million years ago, the snake had swum the seas off Israel. Its mouth would have opened WIDE—like the mouth of today's boas and pythons, which swallow food much bigger than themselves.

Surprisingly, the ancient snake had legs—back legs too short to help it move. No one knows how they were used, but the answer might lie in another museum drawer!

3

Where in the World

A rough green snake spends a lot of its time in the trees.

SNAKES SHOW UP MOST EVERY-WHERE. They live on every continent in the world, except Antarctica. Most find homes where the climate is warm, but some have adapted to cool weather. The common garter snake, for instance, even manages to live in southern parts of Alaska and Canada's Northwest Territories.

Different kinds of snakes settle in different kinds of homes, including damp woods, dry deserts, open grasslands, muggy swamps, and cool streams. Some snakes live right in the water, but most spend the bulk of their time on land or in trees. A

5

few burrow underground.

Snakes don't have a lot of fat to help keep their body temperatures steady. And they don't make much heat of their own. Instead, they lie in sunshine to warm up and head for shade—or sometimes bury themselves in sand—to cool down. Surviving cold winters

Garter snakes take several days to warm up after wintering together in a pit.

can be hard for snakes. That's why many of them enter dens, such as burrows and caves, during the fall. Tucked away, they stay warm enough to live, but not to be active. Their breathing and heartbeats slow down and they sleep deeply—hibernate—for months.

Where winters are especially cold, there may be only a few dens that are deep enough for snakes to avoid freezing. So they share. In some areas, thousands of common garter snakes gather in the same pit each year.

Snakes are surprising! Here are some of the reasons why:

 An eastern screech owl may put a thread snake in its nest to eat up pests, such as tiny insects.

 A snake can keep its mouth closed and stick its tongue out through a notch in its top lip.

 For a time, even a DEAD rattlesnake can snap its jaws shut and release poison.

World of Words

YOU CAN HEAR, SEE, EVEN SMELL SNAKES TALKING. During breeding seasons, female snakes release scents— signals that they're ready to mate. Males can follow these scents over long distances. But if snakes are threatened, their smells have quite a different meaning: "Go away." Glands near their back ends ooze a liquid that can stink for several hours.

Hi-s-s-ing is something most snakes do. The sound can be enough to stop enemies, such as skunks and foxes, in their tracks. The snakes can make their message much stronger by pretending to strike.

Dead—or not! This upside-down hognose snake is probably just pretending.

9

This coral snake's bright bands signal danger, but similar looking non-poisonous snakes might fool you.

The poisonous rattlesnake rattles out warnings with its tail. When jiggled, hard rings at the tip of the tail buz-z-z. Whatever is creeping close to the snake had better dash away—or else.

Snakes that aren't poisonous sometimes shake their tails, too. If they're nestled among dry leaves or loose stones, they can sound a lot like rattlesnakes. And a snake-eater might not stick around to discover the difference.

Bright colors on snakes can act like alarms, frightening or startling their enemies. A coral snake, for instance, is covered in bands of red, white, and black that warn, "I'm poisonous." Snakes such as cottonmouths open their mouths wide and display a warning color inside. And a ringneck snake can startle an animal by exposing red scales beneath its tail.

A hognose snake can be a ham. Bother it and the snake coils up, hisses loudly, and spreads out a "hood" of skin. It rarely bites, but it might strike—with its mouth closed. All this is to say, "Back off."

Don't get the message? The hognose releases a strong smell and displays the purple inside its mouth. Still don't understand? The snake falls on its back—mouth open and tongue hanging out. "Leave me alone," it's saying. "I'm dead anyway."

World in Motion

SNAKES CRAWL, CLIMB, OR SWIM WELL—without any legs. Many snakes can do all three, but some are designed to do one or another best.

A long spine made of many small bones called vertebrae helps snakes move. Each vertebra is connected to a pair of ribs attached, by muscles, to large scales on the snakes' belly. The muscles push and pull these scales as the animals travel.

Snakes normally crawl by bending their bodies into S-shaped curves. They wriggle forward by moving the scales along the back of each curve and pressing against

Pausing to check things out, this fast-moving racer will be gone in a flash.

13

Sidewinders don't travel in the direction they face. They move sideways.

bumps on the ground. Snakes also swim in this S-shaped way, pushing their bodies against the water.

When snakes go climbing, their belly scales catch on the rough bark of trees. Some snakes, such as corn snakes, squeeze themselves into splits in the bark and crawl almost straight up. Tree boas can climb even smooth trees by grabbing a branch with their tails, looping their front ends around a higher branch, and pulling up.

Traveling across loose sand calls for a special method of crawling. A sidewinder, such as a horned rattlesnake, lifts the front of its body and throws it sideways. As that lands, the snake flings a back part, then it tosses the front part again—on and on. That way, the snake can move quickly and keep much of its body off the burning sand.

Super slim, super long snakes called racers earn their name. In the trees or on the ground, they're among the fastest snakes on Earth. As they dart around, hunting for food, racers appear to move like lightning.

The snake's ropelike build creates a false impression, though. Its peak speed is only 6 kilometres (4 miles) an hour—slow for many runners, including you. Still, in the world of snakes, racers are amazingly fast.

World of Senses

Flick. Flick.
The tongue of
a king snake
tests the air
for smells.

NO WINKING. NO BLINKING.
Without lids, snakes can't close their eyes,
even when they're asleep. But they have
spectacles. Rounded, see-through scales
cover and protect their eyes at all times.

Most snakes see well. Their eyes focus
much like cameras do, by moving the
lenses forward and backward. These
lenses are often yellowish—not clear.
The color screens out some of the light
rays and makes it easier for snakes to see
in bright light. The lenses of racers are
among the deepest yellow, helping
these snakes spot fast-moving animals,

17

such as frogs and lizards.

Don't look for outer ears on a snake. It doesn't have any, but some sound vibrations can reach its inner ears. The snake's body can also feel vibrations in the ground. That's how it senses a hiker's footsteps. Still, when it comes to finding food, all these vibrations don't seem to help a snake much. For that, it depends

Pits between the rattlesnake's eyes and nostrils sense heat.

on the tastes and smells that its tongue finds in the air or on the ground.

As a snake hunts, it flicks out its long, forked tongue every few seconds. It sticks the tips of the tongue into two pockets in an organ, called the Jacobson's organ, in the roof of its mouth. This useful tool analyzes tastes and smells, helping the snake find dinner—or sense enemies or mates. And as the snake moves closer to a meal, its tongue might also act as a feeler.

HUNTING BY HEAT

It's great to have pits in your head—if you're a pit viper, such as a rattlesnake, cottonmouth, or copperhead. Nerves in pairs of special pits on the faces of these vipers detect the temperatures of things—living or not.

Hunting in total darkness, a pit viper can sense the difference in warmth between a mouse and the leaves it's hiding under. The snake can tell exactly where the mouse is and strike with deadly accuracy.

19

World Full of Food

As it strikes, the diamondback rattlesnake bares its fangs.

ALL SNAKES EAT ANIMALS—but some are pickier eaters than others. Redbelly snakes, for instance, feed mostly on slugs, and thread snakes gobble up a lot of termites. But many snakes, such as garters, gulp down nearly anything they can—from worms and insects to mice and frogs.

Because snakes can't chew their food, most swallow it whole. It's often bigger around than they are, but snakes are built to handle the job. Their jaws are loosely connected, so they can open WIDE. Their skin stretches, and their ribs spread apart to make room for whatever the snakes take in.

21

A cottonmouth catches a fish for dinner, swallowing it head first.

Small animals that can't fight back are commonly swallowed alive. Others are first killed or made helpless. Snakes such as rattlesnakes have long hollow teeth, called fangs, especially built for injecting poison. These upper teeth normally lie flat, but they flip forward instantly as the snakes strike. Poison stored in the snakes' jaws is injected through the fangs.

Rat snakes, king snakes, boas, and others kill by squeezing. They usually grab an animal by the front of its body, then coil around it— tighter and tighter. They're not trying to crush the animal, just stop it from breathing. Once that happens, the snakes relax their hold and start swallowing—something that can take more than an hour. Depending on the size of the animal and the temperature of the air, digesting the meal can take several days.

LIGHT LUNCH

It sounded like a good plan. Put fake eggs—light bulbs— in chicken nests to encourage hens to lay real eggs there. But a pine snake came along and swallowed two of the fake eggs.

Luckily, the chicken owner noticed the bulbs were missing. When she spotted the snake with its two big lumps, she took it for help. The bulbs were removed through surgery, and the snake survived. Egg shells wouldn't have hurt the pine snake, but the glass bulbs would have!

New World

ROTTEN LOGS CAN MAKE GREAT NESTS FOR SNAKES. So can fallen leaves, sandy soil, and compost heaps. Egg-laying snakes—such as racers and hognose snakes—search for places that are warm, damp, and hidden away. There, they may lay one egg or many. A snake rarely produces more than 50 eggs at a time, but one mud snake in Florida was found with 104!

Mud snakes are one of the few that guard their eggs until they hatch. Most kinds leave their eggs as soon as they've laid them. About 6 to 12 weeks later,

Hatching from its leathery egg, a hognose snake takes its first peek at the world.

After shedding,
a bull snake left
behind a layer
of scaly skin.

little snakes use a special tooth on
their upper jaw to break out of the shell.
The tooth soon falls off.

Many other snakes, such as rosy boas,
garter snakes, and water snakes, don't
need nests at all. They keep their eggs
inside them where their young are well
protected. The new snakes may be born

live or inside their thin-shelled eggs—which they cut with their egg tooth.

Newly arrived snakes look after themselves. They feed mainly on little animals, including insects. Right from birth, rattlesnakes are equipped with poison and fangs for hunting food such as lizards. Snakes grow fast when they're young and have plenty of food, but they never completely stop growing. For small snakes, a lifetime could be as long as 12 years. Large snakes might live to be more than 40.

OLD COAT, NEW COAT

As snakes outgrow and wear out their coats, they grow new ones. Then they simply shed the old coats—their outer layer of skin. But the job takes a while. First, a snake produces a fluid that helps separate the old and new layers. Next, it rubs its head against something firm—pushing back the skin—and gradually wriggles out.

The old skin, now inside out, is left behind. Young snakes usually shed their skin more often than adults do.

Index